Physical and Chemical Reactions

6th Grade Chemistry Book
Children's Chemistry Books

BABY PROFESSOR

EDUCATION KIDS

Speedy Publishing LLC
40 E. Main St. #1156
Newark, DE 19711
www.speedypublishing.com

A chemical reaction occurs when substances undergo a chemical change to create a different substance. A physical reaction occurs when a substance undergoes a physical change, but no chemical reaction. Read on to learn more about these differences and how they affect our lives.

Chemical Change

Chemical changes occur on a much lesser scale. While some experiments will show obvious changes, as in a color change, most of these changes are not evident. The chemical change that takes place as hydrogen peroxide turns into water is not noticeable as both of these liquids are clear. However, what you don't see, is billions of bonds being created and destroyed. In one example, you might observe bubbles of oxygen gas. These bubbles are indication of the chemical changes.

Sugar cubes being melted

When a sugar cube melts, this is considered a physical change since it remains as sugar. A chemical change would result in burning sugar. Fire creates the reaction between oxygen and sugar. The oxygen reacts with the sugar and breaks down its chemical bonds.

Rusting iron occurs when exposed to the oxygen gas in the air. You can see the result as it occurs over a period of time. The changes to its molecules then changes its structure as it is oxidized, resulting eventually into iron oxide. The rusty pipes you might find in an abandoned building is one example of the process of oxidation.

Rusting Metal

Some additional examples of changes which are chemical:

*When iron rusts, iron oxide is formed.
*As gasoline burns, water vapor forms with carbon dioxide.
*As eggs cook, protein molecules are uncoiled and form a network by crosslinking.
*When bread rises, yeast is then converted as its carbohydrates into a carbon dioxide gas.
*Soured milk produces a sour-tasting lactic acid.
*Sun tanning produces vitamin D and melanin.

Physical Change

When you crush an aluminum can after stepping on it, this is known as a physical change. Note that only the shape of the can has been changed, but the matter was not changed since its energy did not change. The molecules remain the same. None of the chemical bonds were broken or created.

As ice melts, a physical change occurs since energy is added. Enough energy was added creating the phase change from a solid to a liquid. Physical actions, including changing the pressure or the temperature causes a physical change. When the ice was melted, no chemical changes occurred. The water molecules remained as water molecules.

As ice melts, a physical change occurs since energy is added. Enough energy was added creating the phase change from a solid to a liquid. Physical actions, including changing the pressure or the temperature causes a physical change. When the ice was melted, no chemical changes occurred. The water molecules remained as water molecules.

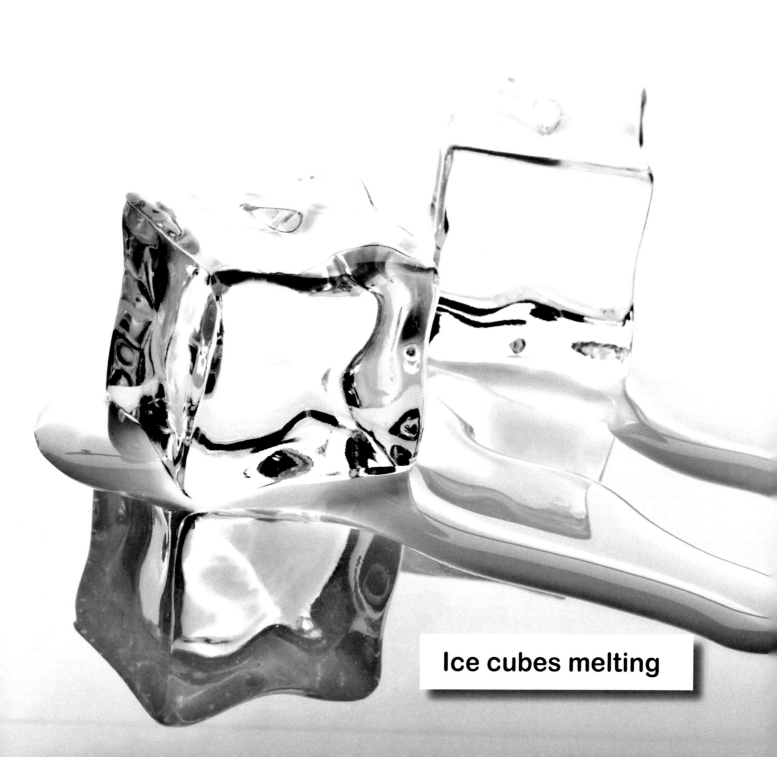

Ice cubes melting

Egg whites whipped

Some additional examples of changes which are physical are:

*As egg whites are whipped, air is forced into its fluid, but the results are now a new substance.
*When a compass needle is magnetized, its group of iron atoms are realigned, but there is no real change in its iron atoms.
*When sugar is dissolved into water, the molecules are dispersed but its molecules remain unchanged.
*When potatoes are diced, the cutting separates the molecules but there is no molecular change.

Classification of these real processes can be difficult. You can break down complex changes into simpler steps. Some of these steps are chemical and some are physical, so overall you might not be able to immediately place them as either physical or chemical. An example would be to boil coffee. This involves a chemical change as its delicate molecules giving the coffee its flavor reacts with the air and becomes a new substance that tastes bitter. However, it also goes through a physical change as the water contained in the coffee goes from a liquid form to a gaseous form.

There are numerous differences between a chemical and a physical change in substances or matters. A physical change does not change what a substance is. During a chemical change when a chemical reaction occurs, this forms a new substance and its energy is either absorbed or released.

An example would be cutting paper in smaller pieces. It takes on a physical change in size and shape, but is still paper. However, when that paper is burned, it breaks up into substances that are no longer paper.

While you can reverse physical changes, you cannot reverse chemical changes without using extraordinary means. An example of a reversing a physical change would be freezing water and returning it to its liquid form by using heat.

You can make sugar water by mixing sugar and water. This would result in a physical change since leaving the sugar out would cause evaporation of the water leaving the sugar crystals. On the other hand, you can't mix up cake ingredients like water, flour, sugar and then cook them and then separate them. Only by extraordinary means could you bring each item back to its original form.

Sugar mixed to water

Chemical reaction results when heat is given off. This is known as an exothermic reaction. An endothermic reaction occurs when the heat is absorbed during a chemical reaction. The pace at which this chemical reaction occurs depends on the pressure of its temperature and the concentration of the involved substances. Catalysts are substances used to accelerate the chemical reaction. An example of a catalyst would be light assisting with film processing.

A chain reaction results when a reaction causes the occurrence of a sequence of reactions.

While you may have seen chemical reactions in science labs, they actually occur all around you every day, no matter where you are or what you are doing. When you eat, your systems use a chemical reaction to break your food down to energy. Rusting metal, burning wood, photosynthesis, and the electricity produced by batteries are some other examples.

Substances used to create a chemical reaction are called reagents and reactants. A substance used or consumed during a reaction is called a reactant. The resulting substance is known as the product.

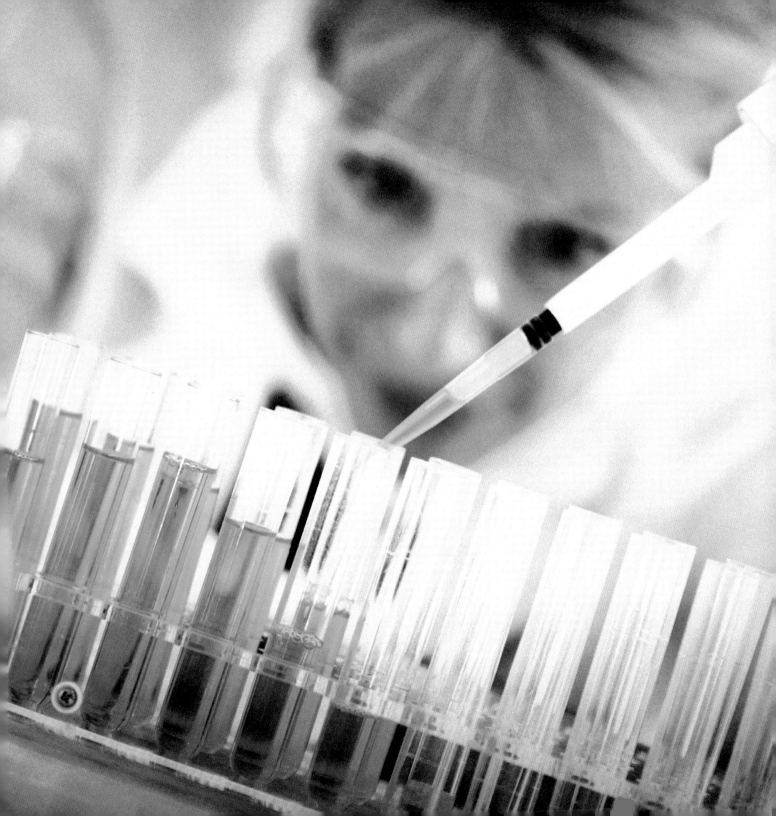

These reactions do not all occur at equal rates. Explosions are an example of a reaction that occurs very quickly, while rusting metal takes place over a long period of time. This is known as the reaction rate. This rate can be altered by adding an energy including electricity, sunlight, or heat. The reaction rate can be increased significantly by adding energy. In addition, increasing the pressure or concentration of the reactants can also increase the speed of the reaction rate.

Types of Reactions

There are several forms of chemical reactions. Here are just a few examples.

Synthesis Reaction

This reaction occurs when two substances join to create a new substance. Its equation is known as A + B --> AB.

Decomposition reaction

This reaction occurs when a complex substance is broken down and forms two separate substances. Its equation is known as AB --> A+ B.

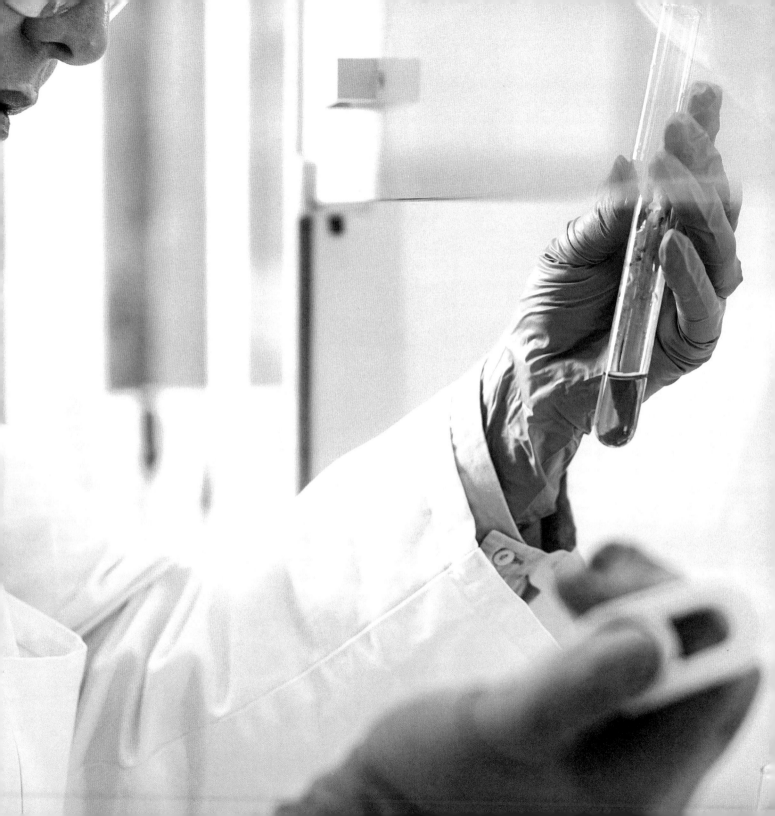

Combustion

This reaction occurs as oxygen is combined with another compound to create water and carbon dioxide. This reaction produces energy resulting in heat.

Single Displacement

This reaction is also known as a substitute reaction. You might think of it as a reaction that takes place when one compound acquires a substance from a different compound. Its equation is known as A + BC --> AC + B.

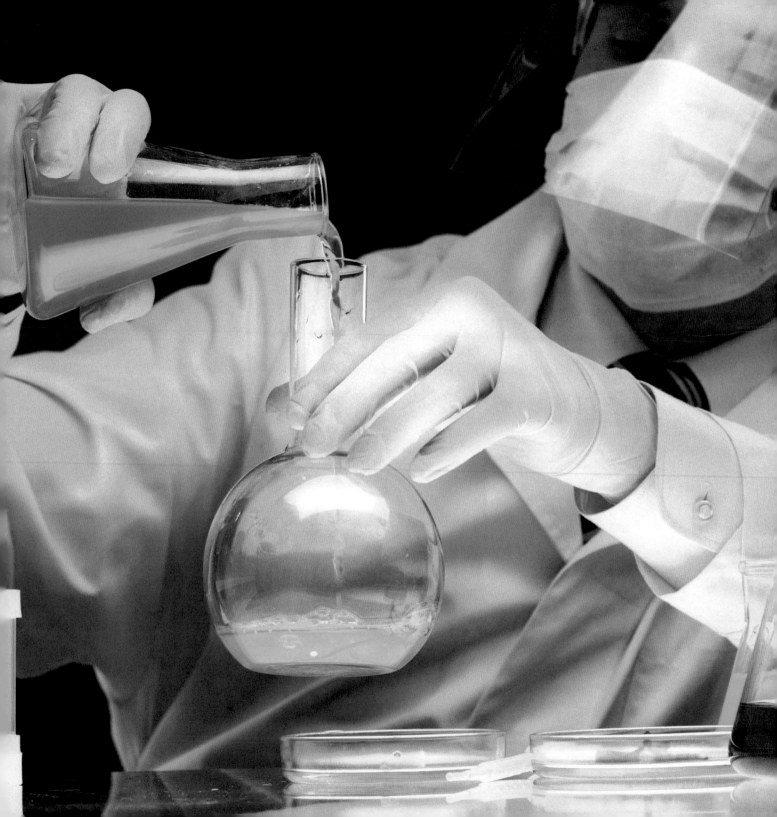

Double Displacement

This reaction is also known as a metathesis reaction. You might think of it as two compounds swapping substances. Its equation is known as AB + CD --> AD + CB.

Photochemical reaction

This reaction involves photons from light. Photosynthesis is an instance of this type of reaction.

In some instances, a third substance may be used to increase the speed or slow down its reaction. A catalyst assists in increasing the speed of the rate of reaction. Unlike different reagents in a reaction, a catalyst is not expended by the reaction. An inhibitor would be used to slow down the rate of reaction.

Isomers

Many chemical changes are very small and occur over a series of steps. The end resulting compounds may have the same number of atoms; however, they will have a different combination or structure of their atoms.

The sugars known as fructose, galactose and glucose each contain six carbon atoms, twelve hydrogen atoms and six oxygen atoms. While they consist of the same atoms, their shapes may vary and are then called isomers. Isomers contain atoms that are bonded in dissimilar orders.

Each of these sugars go through varying reactions due to the differences in the structure of their molecules. Scientists believe that the atoms' arrangement allows for a higher degree of specifity, in particular when these molecules are in living things. Specifity is when these molecules only work in a specific reaction, but not in all of them. An example would be your body using glucose for energy. When you ingest galactose molecules, they have to be converted to glucose in order for your body to use them.

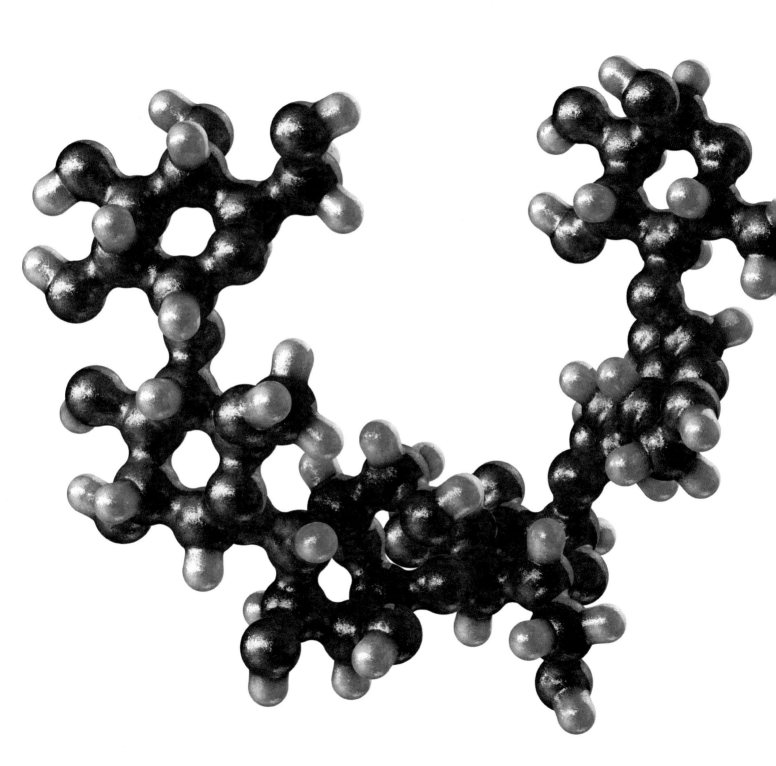

For additional information about the physical and chemical reactions, do some research on the internet and go to the library. You can also ask questions of your teachers, family, and friends.

Made in the USA
Columbia, SC
15 June 2023